Solar Energy Essentials for the Homeowner

Common Questions about Solar Energy for the Home

Blake Webster

Books by Blake Webster

How to Make Money Writing for the Internet

How to Self-Publish Your Book the CreateSpace Way

How to Start Your Online Photography Store

Greener Living Today: Forty Ways to a Greener Lifestyle

How to Start Your Online Affiliate Store: Step-by-Step Guide to Making Money Online

Environmentalists in Action: Profiles of Green Pioneers

Table of Contents

How Do Solar Panels Work?

Solar panels generate electricity that is comparable to a chemical battery or an electric outlet similar to what you would find at your home.

The basic element of solar panels is silicon. When silicon is stripped of all impurities, it makes a great base or platform to support the transmission of electrons. Silicon also has some atomic-level properties which make it idealistic for the creation of solar panels.

Silicon atoms have the ability to fit eight electrons on their band, but only carry four in their natural state. This means there is room for four more electrons. If one silicon atom contacts another silicon atom, each receives the other atom's four electrons. This creates a strong bond, but there is no positive or negative charge because the eight electrons satisfy the atoms' needs. You can think of it as a wash. Silicon atoms can combine for years to result in a large piece of pure silicon. This material described is used to form the plates of solar panels.

How it Works:

Two plates of pure silicon would not generate electricity in solar panels, because they have no positive or negative charge. Remember the wash theory. However to make the effective, solar panels are created by combining silicon with other elements that do have positive or negative charges.

Phosphorus, for example, has five electrons to offer to other atoms. If silicon and phosphorus are combined chemically, the result is a stable eight electrons with an additional free electron tagging along. It can't leave, because it is bonded to the other phosphorus atoms, but it isn't needed by the silicon. Therefore, this new silicon and phosphorus plate is considered to be negatively charged.

In order for electricity to flow, a positive charge must be created. This is achieved in the creation of solar panels by combining silicon with boron, which only has three electrons to offer. A silicon and boron plate still has one spot left for another electron. This means the plate has a positive charge. The two plates are sandwiched together in solar panels, with conductive wires running between them.

With the two plates in place, it's now time to bring in the solar or sunlight need for solar panels. Sunlight sends out many different particles of energy, but the one most meaningful for this explanation is the photon. A photon essentially acts like a moving hammer. When the negative plates of solar cells are pointed at a proper angle to the sun, photons bombard the silicon and phosphorus atoms on the solar plate.

Eventually, the 9th electron is kicked off the outer ring. This electron doesn't remain free for long, since the positive silicon and boron plate draws it into the open spot on its own outer band. As the sun's photons break off more electrons, electricity is generated. The electricity generated by one solar cell is not very impressive, but when all of the plates come together there is enough electricity to power low amperage motors or other electronics.

How Much Energy Can a Solar Panel Generate?

There is no specific answer to the question: 'How much energy can a solar power generate? A large system will absorb a lot of energy and deliver about 50% of it to the storage bank or an appliance; a small one will do the same thing to a lesser degree. A tiny fraction of the world's power is derived from solar power at the present time.

Recapping the statement from above, solar panels produce electricity according to their size, efficiency and how much sunlight they receive. Of course this is also dependent on where you live. Do you get long days filled with sunlight or do you have short days and long nights? For residential properties and small businesses, roof installed panels are a traditional option. Solar panels rated at 100 to 200 watts cover about 10 square feet or 1 square meter. The power you get from a 100-watt solar panel depends on how much sunlight it receives, and on a daily basis the total power is much less than the rated wattage

Specifically, the amount of energy a solar panel can generate is its peak rating (in watts) times the insolation averaged over an entire day (in hours), giving a value in watt-hours. For example:

A 100 watt panel gets an average of 5 hours of good sun/day. It would generate 500 watt-hours, or 0.5 KWH. It might power a desktop computer for a couple hours, or a couple 25 watt CFL's for 10 hours (with the appropriate batteries).

General Misconceptions about power production:

Due to the increase in publicity to go "green" there is a lot of misunderstanding concerning solar energy, as everyone wants to jump on the band wagon, just because it's the right thing to do. To start off the confusion, the advertised capacity of commercial photovoltaic (PV) systems that is specified may be misleading to the consumers. For example, one may not realize that a nameplate rating of system does not represent the wattage it would typically produce in your home. It is just a potential DC power the Photovoltaic array can generate at some ideal sunlight and weather conditions called Standard Test Conditions. When does anyone really ever have standard weather conditions? In reality, your solar panels will operate at STC very rarely. In addition to this, the actual AC output of the system will be 10% to 20% lower than its DC rating due to power losses in the components. In practice, a 5-kilowatt model may probably generate for your home less than 20 kilowatt-hours of electricity over an entire day, which is less than 830 watt averaged over a 24-hour period. Too add insult to injury the manufacturers will use words that are confusing to those who are not electricians, scientists or possess a technical background. As a result, making a decision to purchase a solar power system and selecting the right one that best fits your home or business needs can be challenging.

Solar Energy Essentials for the Homeowner

How Expensive is it to Install Solar Panels?

Homeowners who are considering buying photovoltaic panels should consider their overall needs before investing. For example: is there a desire to have back up batteries for storing electricity? How much of the home do you want to power with your new "green" system? Many manufacturers offer do it yourself packages that make the installation easier and more economical than having professionals come to your residence or business.

An estimated range for upfront costs to include installation, solar panels, inverter box, and high tech wiring is approximately $30-40,000 for a single family house, so long as you are looking to replace grid-based electricity on the entire house with solar energy. The initial investment in solar-energy equipment can be expensive. The cost is high because semiconductor materials used in the manufacture of PV panels are expensive. In 2005, the price of solar panels averaged about $3-$4 USD per watt of installed power. As manufacturers increase production and research continues into less expensive ways to make solar panels, the cost is expected to drop. Costs for PV systems vary depending on what kind of rebates and other financial incentives are available, whether your home is under construction, whether PV panels are integrated into the roof or mounted on top of an existing roof, the size of the system, the price of the components and numerous other factors. Your personal demands will fluctuate this price range higher or lower.

The initial cost does not take into consideration any tax rebates or miscellaneous incentives, which could save you up to eighty percent of the overall cost. Even with an 80% discount, many people might still believe that spending $30,000 – 40,000 on solar panels is too much. That being said, let's look at maintenance cost and energy savings. Studies indicate that your investment could be recouped in about 5-8 years and if you stay in your house longer, then its just like paying yourself.

All in all, despite the initial investment, solar systems can substantially reduce costs of energy over time and add value to your home. Plus, you might be eligible for government financial support as an incentive to buy your solar panels.

As mentioned earlier, you could also experiment with a do-it-yourself solar panel system. But then again when that's all said and done you might be looking at even more money to have someone come and clean up the mess you made, not to mention the potential damage to your roof and electrical system. If this scares you away as I am sure it will, be sure to shop around to get the best bids for a solar panel system purchase and installation, so long as you purchase this from a licensed professional.

How Many Solar Panels do I need to Turn Back the Meter?

Asking a question like this is no different than asking, "How much gas does it take to run a car?" It depends on the car, the miles it is driven, driving habits, and so on. I know someone that has a home close to Canada and it is completely powered by the wind and sun. The solar array is their primary power source, probably providing about 80% of their needs, more in the summer. Although their house is about 1200 square feet, and fairly efficient, their array fits nicely on the roof of the single shed probably taking up 180 square feet, nothing nearly the size of a soccer field. All of their equipment cost just under $15,000, including the batteries. If you can take advantage of net metering in your area, you will not need batteries or charge controllers, but you will need solid utility power from a provider such as BGE (Baltimore MD utility company). The grid becomes your battery in this type of set up. The only downfall is that if the power grid goes down for any reason, your solar array goes with it. So you might find yourself in a situation where the sun is out, and you do not have access to the power in your own solar array. This can be frustrating to new owners.

General consensus says get a subscription to Home Power Magazine, they are the only periodical that gets into the nitti gritty of what you are asking about. You can read about people who have done exactly what you are trying to do in the magazine articles, check out suppliers websites that advertise there and learn a great deal. In the end, you might decide not to get involved, and that's fine, but at least you will be well informed.

If you're a contractor yourself and can do some basic wiring, I would suggest you start by getting one panel, a couple golf cart batteries and some DC breakers and switches and set up your own 12 volt power system. We have some friends who did 12 years ago, even put 12 volt outlets in all the rooms. They still work today and continue to be perfect for small electronics and lights. If you subscribe to Home Power, you can go online to their website and look up archived articles from years past. Use their search engine to look up, "Starting a home based solar kit", if you want to see it. It also may be wise to go to an energy fair if you're really interested after looking all this up.

For comparison purposes, I will give you the specs on the home system we mentioned above. This is the equipment necessary to run that home, with a little help from the utility company. Their electric bills average just under $5 per month.

Solar: 14 Kyocera KC-120 panels, total solar power 1.6 KW
Wind: Southwest Windpower H-40,. max power 900 watts
Inverter: Trace Engineering SW-4024 4000 watts continuous, 10,000 watts surge limit
Batteries: Trojan L-16 model 360's, 20 total storing 1801

amp hours at 24 volts DC

How to Determine the Number of
Solar Panels for your Home

With a few easy steps you too can calculate how many solar panels you need for your home.

Two Important Questions to uncover are:

What is the number of **Watt-hours (Wh)** you may to produce on a given day?
What is the **insolation** value at your location.

Watt Hours:

The watt-hour (Wh) is a unit of energy equivalent to one watt of power expended for one hour of time. The watt-hour is not a standard unit in any formal system, but it is commonly used in electrical applications.

Determining your Watt Hours (Wh) is the most essential aspect of accurately estimating how big of a system you will need. Basically you are determining how many Watts of solar panel generating capacity you will need. If you plan to tie your solar panel layout directly to the utility grid to offset your costs, start by looking at your electric utility bill for the kilowatt-hours (kWh) you use in one month. Please note, this fluctuates month to month, so if you are looking at a bill from the spring where you may have had your windows open to help naturally cool your home, you might want to calculate your average monthly usage from the historical information found on the previous eleven months electric bills. People often choose to offset a certain portion of their average electricity usage based on their budget.

If you will not be connected to the utility grid and you will be producing all of your own electricity, the Watt-hours or kWh number becomes even more important. For any off-grid cabin, home, or office it is strongly recommended completing a detailed loads list. The loads list outline can be found via conducting a basic Google search for "loads list for solar energy".

Insolation:

Insolation is a nontraditional word for the number of hours in a day that a solar panel will produce its projected voltage. Remember, all the day's sunshine counts toward this total, not just the brightest hours, and not every hour of sunlight counts equally. When the sun is low in the sky, a solar panel facing it doesn't produce as much energy as it would at noon. An alternate way to explain this would be to imagine that you crammed all the day's sunlight, both weak and strong, into equal hours of "peak" sunshine; your results would be the "sun hours", or insolation number.

Also remember every geographic location is different, in your locale, while the sun may be up for ten or so hours during a January day, not all that light is strong enough to be counted at full value, so the insolation value in your area may be closer to 2 sun hours. In alternate calculations, we use average insolation values taken from years of data that has been collected by astronomers or "green" research laboratories. To recap, insolation varies by location as well as by month. If you're planning a year-round solar electric system, the annual average insolation value will give you a good starting point for your estimate. If you only plan to use the solar panel system seasonally, then use the insolation values for those months only. As mentioned earlier, **insolation** tables and research can be found on the internet to help with these calculations.

Calculations:

Step 1:
Take the number of Watt-hours you want to produce in one day and divide it by the insolation value, in hours.

Ex. 6 Wh / 3 hours = 2 Watts

Step 2:
Allow for the normal energy losses and inefficiencies in a solar electric system. Do this by increasing the number of Watts you found in Step 1 by 30%.

Ex. 2 Watts x 1.3 = 2.6 Watts

Now you know you can look for a 10.4 Watt system in order to produce, on average, 8 Watts per day.

** Note these numbers help to express the formula and are not exact to your individual system.

Blake Webster

What is the Cheapest Approach to Purchasing Solar Panels?

There are three approaches one can use when purchasing solar panels.

Purchase solar panels from an authorized retailer.
Purchase the solar panels used or second hand.
Do It Yourself (building them from scratch)

Purchasing from a retailer or supplier:

The best way to get brand new solar panels is straight from the manufacturer or the manufacturer's main supplier if possible. Buying from the manufactures will cut down on vendors' profit margins and these companies are usually much more reliable when it comes to support with warranty issues.

It is suggested that you buy from within your county, as measurements are different and if an issue arises you can easily return the panels without extreme shipping charges. On the front end look for deals or suppliers who offer free shipping options

New solar panels and other equipment should come with a warranty, along with an indication of the quality, specifically, the manufacturing and parts being used. That being said, you should check with the company to see how such a warranty would be utilized if the need were to arise.

It is also necessary to be wary of possible scams. Several websites and infomercials have claimed to be selling solar paint. These sites are almost certainly scams, as commercially available paint on coatings that could produce electricity are still years away from production, and is nothing more than shiny black paint in a can.

Used or Second Hand Panels

Used solar panels can be an excellent deal, but there are a few things to investigate;

How old is it?
The age of the solar panel will affect its productivity, especially if it is a thin film panel. The efficiency of used thin film panels can be as low as 6%. On the other hand, if it is a monocrystaline or polycrystalline panel its age should not negatively affect its operation.

Is it structurally sound?
If the panel is not sealed properly you will find moisture condensing on the inside of the glass or plastic cover. This will have a significant impact on its performance, and end up being a decorative piece versus an energy producer.

Does it provide a steady current flow of wattage throughout the day?
If the panel exhibits various outputs of voltage, or the voltage drops in the brightest part of the day, then it can be assumed that there are issues with corrosion or other internal

damage.

Do It Yourself:

The DIY panel was introduced in order to give people a cheaper option to incorporate solar energy into their home

If you want more information regarding do it yourself solar panel, you can go online and search different sites that offer DIY solar power kits.

One thing to keep in mind is that it costs more to build an expandable system. If you start out with a 1 kW system then add to it slowly, it is going to cost much more than building the whole unit at once.

12 kW is a large system for a house. If saving money is a concern, find out if there are any conservation measures you can do first? If you haven't done so yet, it's worth getting a professional installer to look at your house and energy bills and bid on a system. You can always decline, but at least that will realistically size your system.

Also, large installers can get panels much more cheaply than a consumer can, no matter what, so it's possible that it would cost less to have someone provide the whole package versus buying all of the parts yourself.

Will the Electric Company Pay me Back for the Electricity I Generate?

Yes, it has been confirmed through various sources that the utility company will credit you for whatever electric energy you generate and feed back into the power grid. To provide a visual example, think of it as spinning your electric meter backwards. (Almost like turning back the clock for daylight savings time.) However to make this work, you must have a system that can comply with the law, and feed excess energy back into the grid. There are some solar panel systems that are only created to serve your residence and not supply excess energy to the grid.

If you are fortunate to generate enough energy to "give back" then you will most likely be required to enter into a contract that supports you as a supplier with your utility or electric company.

Contracts are not universal throughout the country and may differ by company. The only place for accurate information is with your specific utility company and what they have to offer. This may be somewhat superseded by state regulations or mandates.

Time of use rates apply to consumers who have alternate rates for off peak usage than daytime usage. For example, in California where peak daytime rates may be as high as 30 cents per KWh nighttime rates may be as low as 5 or 6 cents. Normally what is expressed is a 50% reduction for nighttime usage. You may be required to have two separate meters, so don't let this be a shock.

The rate the utility company is willing to offer for your electricity is also found in your agreement. It will be a different rate for different geographical locations. However, it would be highly irregular that you would be able to offer solar based electricity during the night. Solar panels and the creation of electricity is usually a daytime product and that is also the time when utility companies need it the most. It is highly unlikely that you will be paid the sheet rate for peak electricity, but it could be based on the sheet rate. In some places this is regulated to be the same rate you would have to pay to buy the electricity.

Can I Make my own Solar Panels?

Yes, this is possible with adequate research and know-how.

Building solar panels at home is basically about assembling photovoltaic cells and putting them into a homemade box. Boxes can be constructed from metals, plastic or wood. Once the electricity demands of the system are known, the correct amount of solar cells can be assembled accordingly. Solar cells are sold in a wide variety of sizes, ranging in price from $6 to $40, and can be matched to a consumers desired needs. If the system is to power an outdoor fish tank's water pump, only a few small cells will be needed. If there is desire to power a kitchen, complete with a power-hungry microwave oven and electric range, a few hundred big cells assembled into a few larger panels will probably be needed. In any case, the combined output of the cells must at least match and should probably exceed the demands of the system.

Building the Frame:

One should start by blueprinting a plan for the panel. After choosing the size of the solar cells, a square or rectangular outline should be drawn showing their arrangement. Be sure to include some cushion space between the individual cells. This will increase the overall size of the panel. Using these measurements, a back or platform can be cut from ½ -inch or slightly thinner plywood. This platform could even be cut or framed with scrap wood, depending on preference. After initial creation of the platform, holes should be drilled into the frame for ventilation. A non-conductive, porous substrate like pegboard or cork should be attached to the backing. The best way to do this is with wood glue, reinforced by some screws in the corners. The whole box should be primed and painted. The cells are supposed to last for 18 to 26 years, so make your box heavy duty so it can weather the conditions.

Drop those Solar Cells In:

Use a thick marking pen to draw lines that will be used as a cell-placement guide. Most solar cells are made with tabs, so they can be soldered together. For ease of assembly and installation, several of these should be soldered into units of blocks. They can also be done as rows, columns or squares. The cell rows can then be attached into place on the substrate using non-conductive silicon caulking similar to a glue.

Wire It Together:

Every cell will have a pair of wires running out of it. These wires should be identified as the positive and negative leads, spliced and joined with wire nuts. To keep everything tidy and organized, the wires should be glued inside the box with caulk, similar to a silicon compound used in the earlier step. By splicing and bridging the wiring together, all the solar cells are tied together into a single wire. Run this wire run out of the box, through a hole which you then must seal with caulk. Remember, this box needs to be water and weather proof.

Last Step:

Finally, cut a piece of Plexiglas to fit the front of the box that you have just created. You will need to screw it into place, again, making sure to make it tight enough to keep the weather out. Your homemade solar panel is now ready to be positioned so that it can catch the maximum amount of sunlight and connected to a charge controller which controls the voltage and current coming from the solar panels to the storage mechanism (batteries).

How much Electricity is Produced from Solar Energy?

Solar panels produce electric power according to their size, efficiency and how much sunlight they receive, so the answer to this question depends on many things. For home and business owners, roof-mounted panels are usually the norm. Solar panels rated at 100 to 200 watts cover about 10 square feet. The power you get from a 100-watt solar panel depends on how much sunlight it receives, and on a daily basis the total power is much less than the rated wattage.

So of course, if you had a 7,000 square foot lot completely filled with solar panels, that would help to produce and store more electricity versus the panels mounted on your 700 square foot roof.

Professional engineers design solar panels to attract and convert the maximum amount of energy out of sunlight. Most of the sunlight that hits a solar panel is not converted into electricity, convertible sunlight has to be the right wavelength (color) and it has to be absorbed, not reflected. Typical panels available for home or business use have efficiencies less than 20 percent. This means that only 20 percent of the power of the sunlight reaching the solar panel is converted to electricity. This is already figured into the rated wattage for a solar panel, often times found on the spec sheet. Electric power is rated over time by watts per hour, or kilowatt hours.

The amount of power a solar panel can achieve and the power it delivers are two different measures. If a given panel is rated at 180 watts, then it will perform up to that level in the brightest sunlight. However, unless you live on the Equator, your solar panel will not receive that much sunlight, it's just not practical. The amount of sunlight that reaches the ground in your region (called insolation, averaged in watts per square meter, divided by standard bright sunlight (1000 watts per square meter) will tell you what portion of the rated wattage your panel will produce.

An easier method is to ask your local vendor about the number of peak sun hours your location receives each day. If they are selling these panels and are knowledgeable in the field, they should be able to tell you in an instant what the number of local sun hours is. A peak sun hour is one hour of 1,000 watts per square meter sunlight Most locations in the United States receive less than six sun hours per day. You can predict how much power a given solar panel can generate by multiplying the watt rating of a solar panel by the number of peak sun hours for your location. Note that the sun hours will vary by season, and are lowest during the winter.

All in all, there are a few other factors that need to be considered when determining your solar panels maximum potential.

Is your panel in full sunlight? Is it positioned properly to attain the maximum exposure?

Cloud cover will reduce the power by up to 30 percent or more. Snow and dust will limit the amount of light that reaches the panel and reduce power output.

What is the Best Roof Angle for Solar Panels?

To get the most from solar panels, you need to point them in the direction that captures the most amount of sunlight. That being said, there are a number of variables in figuring out the best direction.

This advice applies to any type of solar panel or array that gets energy from sunlight. Most common solar arrays, or panels, are fixed, or have a tilt that can be adjusted seasonally. Some of the more complex systems have automatically adjusting Panels that track the movement of the sun throughout the day. These panels can receive 10% more energy in winter and up to 40% more energy in summer than the fixed panels do.

Solar panels should always face the south if you are in the northern hemisphere, or north if you are in the southern hemisphere. Remember, true north is not the same as magnetic north. If you are using a compass to set your panels, you need to correct for the difference, which varies from place to place. It is suggested that you search the web for "magnetic declination" to find the correction for your location.

Tilt Angle:

As mentioned earlier to capture the maximum amount of sunlight to your solar panels over a year, you may need to adjust them in accordance to the season in your geographic location. However, generally speaking, the panels should be tilted at an angle approximately equal to a site's latitude and facing within 15° of due south. To maximize the performance during the winter months, the panels should be tilted 15° more than the latitude angle. For longer hours of sunlight, usually occurring in the summer time and to optimize summer performance, 15° less than the latitude angle is suggested. At any given instant, the panels will output maximum available power when pointed directly at the sun.

To compare the energy output of your panels to the optimum value, you will need to know the site's latitude, and the actual tilt angle of your panels, which may be the slope of your roof if your array is flush-mounted. If your solar panels tilt is within 15° of the latitude angle, you can expect a decrease of 5% or less in your system's annual energy production. If your solar panel's tilt is greater than 15° off the latitude angle, the reduction in your system's annual energy production may go down by as much as 15% from its peak available value. During winter months or shorter days with less hours of sunlight, or at higher latitudes, the reduction will be greater.

Azimuth Angle and Magnetic Declination:

If a south-facing roof is unavailable, or the total solar panel cluster is larger than the area of a south-facing roof section, an east or west-facing surface is the next best option. Be aware that solar power output decreases proportionally with a horizontal angle, greater than 15° from due south. The decrease in annual power output from a latitude-tilted east or west-facing array may be as much as 15% or more in the lower latitudes or as much as 25% or more in the higher latitudes of the United States. Avoid directing your tilted solar panels northwest, north or northeast, as you'll get little power output.

Magnetic declination, the angle difference between magnetic south and true solar south, must also be taken into account when determining proper solar array orientation.

Are there Drawbacks to Solar Energy?

In general, there are many more advantages to using solar energy then there are disadvantages, but here are a few for review.

Cost - One of the main disadvantages to implement a solar panel system is the initial cost of the equipment (panels) that are used to attract and convert the sunlight into energy. Solar energy technologies still remain a costly alternative as compared to the use of readily available fossil fuel technologies. All things constant, as the price of solar panels decreases, we are likely to see an increase in the use of solar cells to generate electricity.

Installation and Space - Another objective topic for review is the installation process. The installation of solar panels requires a large area for a desired system to be efficient in providing a source of electricity. The location of solar panels can affect performance, due to possible obstructions from the surrounding buildings or landscape. This is a disadvantage in areas where space is short, or expensive, such as townhomes, condos, and inner cities.

Pollution – This can also be a disadvantage to solar panels, as pollution can degrade the efficiency of photovoltaic cells. Similarly, clouds can also provide the same effect, as they can reduce the energy of the sun's rays, causing a decrease in converted energy.

Uncontrollable Factors - Weather, location, time of day and time of year may all have an impact on the amount of solar energy your solar arrays can produce. Solar panels are useful when the sun is shining, and during the night, your solar equipment will be useless; however the use of solar battery chargers can help to reduce the effects of this disadvantage. On cloudy days, when a limited amount of sunlight reaches the earth, only a minimal amount of solar energy is collected. Locations that are far from the equator, where winter days are quite short, and locations that have generally cloudy weather may be impractical places for generating solar energy.

Potential Release of Hazardous Waste - Solar photovoltaic panels or arrays may contain hazardous materials that could be released when a panel is broken or disposed of improperly. Think about how dangerous it would be if a tree were to fall on your roof and break 1,000 sq. feet of solar panels.

Visual Appearance – Plain and simple, beauty is in the eye of the beholder, what one may think is beautiful another may think is hideous. This drawback or disadvantage is open for criticism, but the general consensus is that solar panels are not very astatically pleasing when placed on a roof of a residential home. However over time and with new advances, there may be a day, when solar panels are built into shingles and can deliver the same net effect as the large panels, without the eye sore.

Are Solar Batteries Safe?

As discussed earlier, there is some hazardous waste that can be released if a solar panel is broken and not discarded of properly, and this would also stand true for solar batteries, or batteries of any kind. All that being said, generally speaking solar batteries are safe.

Solar batteries are really deep cycle batteries that provide energy storage for solar, wind and other renewable energy systems. Different from a car battery, a deep cycle battery is capable of surviving prolonged, repeated and deep discharges which are typical in renewable energy systems that are "off the grid" which means to be 100% self-sufficient and not hooked up to the utility company.

Solar Batteries (Deep Cycle Batteries) are a key component in a stand-alone solar energy system. This is also the same type of battery you would use if you are installing a wind, or hydro electric system that will be tied to your utility grid. Having these batteries will help prevent you from experiencing an interruption in power due to the lack of natural energy being produced, i.e. no sunlight or wind. Without deep cycle batteries, you can only use power at the time you produce it, not very practical for the use of electricity during the evening.

In renewable energy systems, deep cycle batteries provide the energy storage for your system. Unlike your car battery, deep cycle batteries that are used in renewable energy systems are meant to be drained and then recharged over time repeatedly. To prolong battery life, most manufacturers suggest limiting the depth of discharge to about 20%. (That means the deep cycle batteries will be at 80% capacity or better.) The general rule of thumb is at minimum, do not allow the batteries to be discharged below 50%. Often a power inverter will have a low voltage disconnect feature that will disconnect loads at a given set point. Low voltage alarms can provide audible warnings as well. Ammeters, Voltmeters and Battery Monitors can help better maintain deep cycle battery health and provide statistics about the overall health of the system.

Deep cycle batteries come in many sizes: from batteries that are less than ten pounds to ones that weigh over two hundred pounds. They can be small enough to fit in your purse or large enough where you couldn't pick them up without help. Generally the size and weight correspond with the designated amp hours of storage. If you need a lot of energy storage, make sure that you have enough space in your home or office to accommodate the necessary battery size that will be required to run your electric devices.

Whether you have one battery or a control room of forty, proper storage is essential. Enclosures for Deep Cycle Batteries can provide a neat and safe way to contain the batteries or you can build your own battery box. Often people add optional Ventilators/Battery Fans that can vent the hydrogen gas that is naturally exhausted by the deep cycle batteries charging. The level of hydrogen gas that could be emitted has not been proven harmful and is not considered a concern for implementing solar energy systems.

If we have Solar Energy will we still have Power at Night?

The big problem with solar power is an obvious one, the sun isn't always shining and it is not present at all during the night. At nighttime or on cloudy days, solar panels simply can't access the sun's energy.

The solution is a simple one: Store the sun's energy so you can use it when the sun's not available. Unfortunately, implementing that solution has been extremely problematic - - until a recent breakthrough made solar-energy storage a realistic option for the energy industry.

There are three different solutions one could use. On a smaller scale you could use traditional batteries that help to store energy that has been produced by the solar panels, or a grid tie in.

Battery Banks

One way solar power storage can be accomplished is by using a battery bank to store the electricity generated by the PV solar power system. A battery solar power storage system is used in a grid-tied PV system with battery backup and stand-alone PV systems.

The major components of a battery solar power system are:

Charge Controller: Prevents the battery bank from overcharging by interrupting the flow of electricity from the PV panels when the battery bank is full.

Battery Bank: A group of batteries wired together. The batteries are similar to car batteries, but designed specifically to endure the type of charging and discharging they'll need to handle in a solar power system.

System Meter: Measures and displays your solar PV systems performance and status.

Main DC Disconnect: A DC rated breaker between the batteries and the inverter. This allows the inverter to be quickly disconnected from the battery bank for service.

Grid Tie In

The second type of PV solar power system is a grid-tied PV system. This system can actually use the grid as its solar energy storage system. This is done using net-metering. When you produce excess solar electricity, you send it to the grid and your electric meter rolls backwards. Later on, at night for example, when your system is not producing electricity, you can pull electricity from the grid and your electric meter will roll forward. You are essentially using the grid to store your solar electricity!

Salt Approach
Because most salts only melt at high temperatures and do not turn to vapor until they get considerably hotter, subsequently they can then be used to store a lot of the sun's energy as heat. Simply, during the day use the sunlight to

heat up the salts and then put those molten salts in proximity to water via a heat exchanger. Hot steam can then be utilized to turn turbines without losing too much of the original absorbed solar energy.

The salts—a mixture of sodium and potassium nitrate, otherwise used as fertilizers allow enough of the sun's heat to be stored that so that it can have enough electricity for nearly eight hours after the sun starts to set.

What are the Two Main Types of Solar Panels used Today?

A solar panel is a box like platform that contains a packaged, connected assembly of photovoltaic cells. The solar panel can be used as a component of a larger photovoltaic system to generate and supply electricity in commercial and residential applications. Each panel is rated by its DC output power under standard operating conditions. All that being said, what might be good for a commercial building might not be the best idea for a residential building when you consider cost, available mounting space, etc. The requirements for residential and commercial are different in that the residential needs are simple and can be packaged so that as solar cell technology progresses, the other base line equipment such as the battery, inverter and voltage sensing transfer switch still need to be compacted and unitized for residential use. Commercial use, depending on the size of the service will be limited in the photovoltaic cell arena, and more complex parabolic reflectors and solar concentrators are becoming the dominant technology. Studies indicate there are two types of solar panels that have reached mainstream production and sales, these are Momocrystalline Silicon Panels and Polycrystalline Silicon Panels.

Momocrystalline Silicon (Mono-silicon or single sillcon) Momocrystaline silicon is used in the manufacturing of solar cells, which are what your highest performing solar panels are made of. Since, solar cells are less demanding than microelectronics, monocrystaline solar cells are a preference to use when creating panels for public distribution. Monocrystalline solar cells can achieve 17% efficiency whereas other types of less expensive cells including thin film and polycrystalline are only capable of achieving around 10% efficiency. Efficency is very important and getting an extra 70% makes a world of difference when you are trying to heat a personal residence or business. Few solar charger companies use monocrystalline solar panels because of the higher cost to produce the solar cells, although these higher efficiency products are starting to surface as consumers demand more efficient products.

Polycrystalline Silicon
Polycrystalline solar panels are designed to have lower silicon levels than monocrystalline panels. As a result, that makes them less expensive to produce, but as one would expect they are also slightly less efficient. Growth of the photovoltaic solar industry was initially limited by the supply of the polysilicon material. However, as solar energy and "going green" became more of a hot topic in 2006, over half of the world's supply of polysilicon was being used for production of renewable electricity solar power panels. As of 2008 only twelve factories were known to produce solar-grade polysilicon, it is estimated that this number has increased by now (2012) especially with the tax credits associated with utilizing renewable energy source.

If you are interested in checking out some of the top ten manufacturers measured by shipments, they are the following:

1. Suntech
2. First Solar
3. Sharp Solar
4. Yingli
5. Canadian Solar
6. Trina Solar
7. Hanwha Solarone
8. Sunpower
9. Renewable Energy Corporation
10. Solarworld

Online Solar Energy Resources

Solar Energy International

For 21 years, Solar Energy International has been dedicated to hands-on labs, online solar training, and renewable energy education. SEI also works with grassroots and development organizations to promote sustainability and improve quality of life worldwide through viable outreach programs

http://www.solarenergy.org/

The International Solar Energy Society

ISES has been serving the needs of the renewable energy community since its founding in 1954. A UN-accredited NGO present in more than 50 countries, the Society supports its members in the advancement of renewable energy technology, implementation and education all over the world.

https://www.ises.org/ises.nsf

Clean Energy Research Center

The USF Clean Energy Research Center's fundamental investigations into new environmentally clean energy sources and systems (hydrogen, fuel cells, solar energy conversion and biomass utilization) meet the needs of power and energy producers and the transportation sector through multi-disciplinary research, technical and infrastructure development and information transfer.

http://cerc.eng.usf.edu/

Nextronex

Nextronex is a solar component manufacturing company that develops and sells utility-scale grid-tie inverter systems for photovoltaic installations.

Nextronex is dedicated to becoming known as the premier provider in utility scale solar inverters, supplying energy maximization systems for photovoltaic array systems across the country and around the world.

http://www.nextronex.com/default.asp

Texas Solar Energy Society

Texas Solar Energy Society is a non-profit organization with a long history of solar and renewable energy outreach and education. Founded in 1976, they have been serving Texas for years

http://www.txses.org/solar/content/about-txses

Renewable Energy World

Explore renewable energy news, jobs, events, companies, and more.

http://www.renewableenergyworld.com/rea/home

Solar Server

Since 1999, SolarServer with up to 16.000 users per day is the most visited German Solar-Portal.

A Monthly average of 210,000 hits, more than 1.5 million pages viewed and persistent top rankings in Google for important keywords demonstrates the attractiveness of the portal.

http://www.solarserver.com/

The Refrigeration School, Inc

Online Training for Solar Panel Installation

Solar Panel installation and maintenance is a growing career field and which is due in part to the country's recent investment in green energy systems. Solar panel installers are responsible for installing and maintaining these alternative energy sources that work through the sun's energy. Job growth has been increasing steadily and is expected to continue to grow because the need for alternative energy sources has been increasing, as well.

The website below will help you to get started in this exciting field and help you to achieve the training you need to succeed.

http://www.refrigerationschool.com/articles/get-online-training-to-install-solar-panels.html

Reference

1. http://www.wisegeek.com/how-do-solar-panels-work.htm

2. http://www.ehow.com/about_5398329_much-power-solar-panel-generate.html

3. http://answers.yahoo.com/question/index?qid=20090411112300AAR4kuf

4. http://www.factsaboutsolarenergy.us/

5. http://ezinearticles.com/?How-Much-Power-Does-Solar-Power-Energy-Generate?&id=4983883

6. http://solarpanelspower.net/solar-panels/solar-panels-cost

7. http://www.trustyguides.com/solar-panels2.html

8. http://answers.yahoo.com/question/index?qid=20100625092340AA4dKwb

9. http://www.altestore.com/howto/Solar-Electric-Power/Getting-Started/How-Many-Solar-Panels-do-you-need-in-your-Solar-Array/a88/

10. http://searchcio-midmarket.techtarget.com/definition/watt-hour

11. http://answers.yahoo.com/question/index?qid=20090816140

232AAUCtK7

12. http://ezinearticles.com/?DIY-Solar-Panels---The-Cheapest-Way-to-Get-Solar-Power&id=3807230

13. http://www.green-planet-solar-energy.com/cheap-solar-panels.html

14. http://answers.yahoo.com/question/index?qid=20100601205844AA7v0pX

15. http://www.zjucnc.org/solar-electric/does-the-electric-company-pay-me-for-solar-energy

16. http://www.ehow.com/how-does_5002015_how-can-own-solar-panels.html

17. http://www.ehow.com/about_5398329_much-power-solar-panel-generate.html

18. http://www.macslab.com/optsolar.html

19. http://answers.yahoo.com/question/index?qid=20080523115721AAPln0s

20. http://www.ehow.com/about_5081441_benefits-drawbacks-solar-energy.html

21. http://www.clean-energy-ideas.com/articles/disadvantages_of_solar_energy.html

22. http://www.livestrong.com/article/131232-drawbacks-solar-energy/

23. http://chemistry.about.com/od/elementfacts/a/hydrogen.htm

24. http://www.altestore.com/store/Deep-Cycle-Batteries/c434/

25. http://science.howstuffworks.com/environmental/greentech/energy-production/solar-energy-night.htm

26. http://www.scientificamerican.com/article.cfm?id=how-to-use-solar-energy-at-night

27. http://www.solar-energy-at-home.com/how-is-solar-energy-stored.htm

28. http://www.scientificamerican.com/article.cfm?id=how-to-use-solar-energy-at-night

29. http://en.wikipedia.org/wiki/Monocrystalline_silicon

30. http://howsolarworks.1bog.org/different-types-of-solar-panels/

31. http://en.wikipedia.org/wiki/Polycrystalline_silicon

32. http://en.wikipedia.org/wiki/Solar_panel